ZIG ZAG

TURN OFF THE TELLY!

by Charlie Gardner
illustrated by Barbara Nascimbeni

Evans

"Turn off the telly,"
said Mum. "Do it now!"

"But what shall we do,
and how?"

"Try a board game!"
"Board games are boring."

"A jigsaw!"
"Jigsaws get us snoring."

So we find a box, the
one for the telly.
It's dark inside and
a little bit smelly.

We sit and we
think of the telly
we're missing…

15

…Aqua Boy, Red Harry, and princesses wishing.

18

"I'll be Aqua Boy and you be
his pet shark.
Let's save Princess Coral
before it gets dark."

19

We zoom through the
ocean in our sonic sub…

...and fight the giant octopus that lives in the tub.

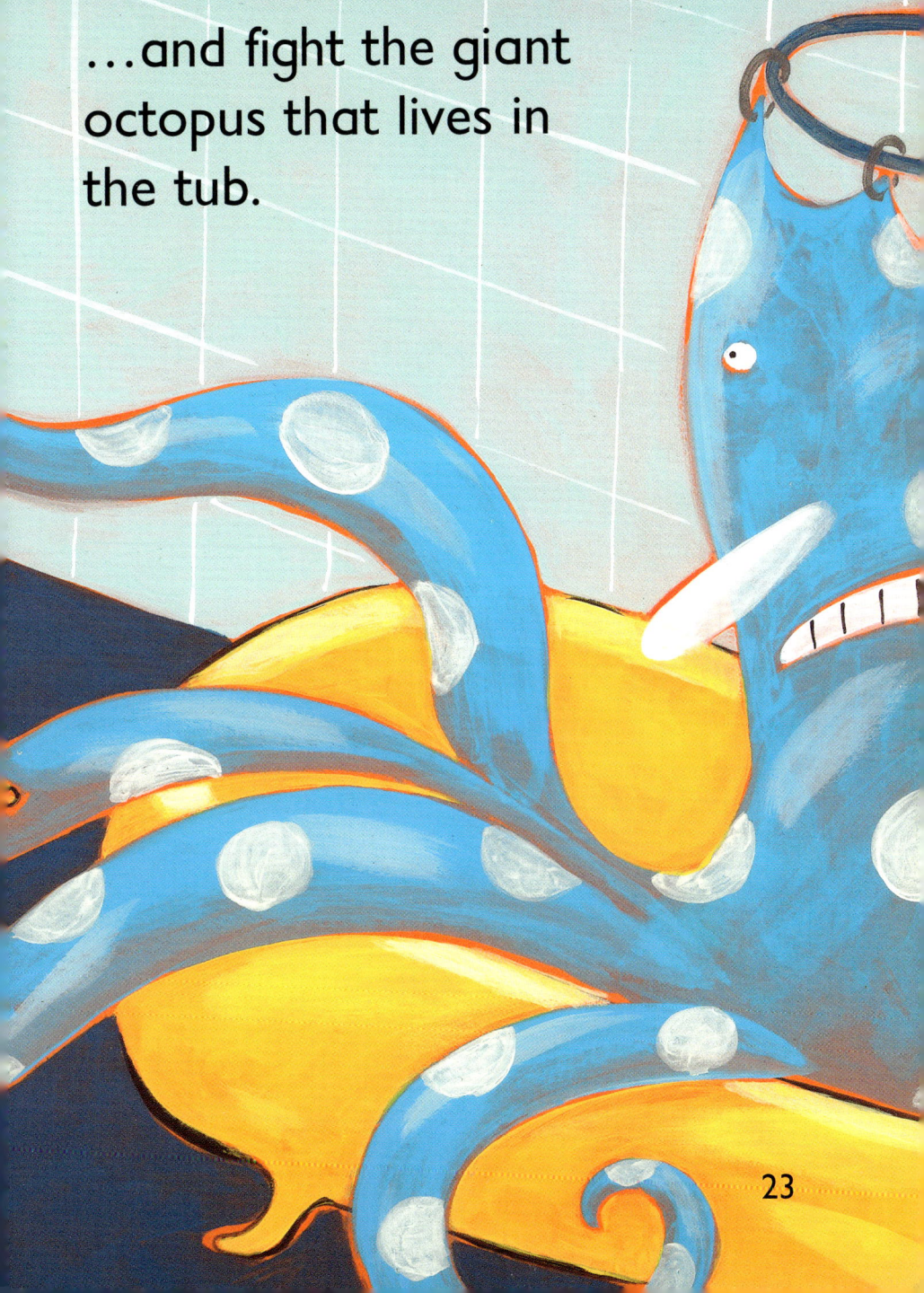

Past the strange vacuum
monster next to the door,
past the huge sea slug that
lives on the floor.

"Look out for the jellyfish with stings in its belly!" Then we find Princess Coral…

27

...downstairs –
watching telly!

28

"Turn off the telly!
Turn it off NOW!"

Why not try reading another ZigZag book?

Dinosaur Planet
by David Orme and Fabiano Fiorin

ISBN 0 237 52667 0

Tall Tilly
by Jillian Powell and Tim Archbold

ISBN 0 237 52668 9

Batty Betty's Spells
by Hilary Robinson and Belinda Worsley

ISBN 0 237 52669 7

The Thirsty Moose
by David Orme and Mike Gordon

ISBN 0 237 52666 2

The Clumsy Cow
by Julia Moffat and Lisa Williams

ISBN 0 237 52656 5

Open Wide!
by Julia Moffatt and Anni Axworthy

ISBN 0 237 52657 3

Too Small
by Kay Woodward and Deborah van de Leigraaf

ISBN 0 237 52777 4

I Wish I Was An Alien
by Vivian French and Lisa Williams

ISBN 0 237 52776 6

The Disappearing Cheese
by Paul Harrison and Ruth Rivers

ISBN 0 237 52775 8

Terry the Flying Turtle
by Anna Wilson and Mike Gordon

ISBN 0 237 52774 X

Pet To School Day
by Hilary Robinson and Tim Archbold

ISBN 0 237 52773 1

The Cat in the Coat
by Vivian French and Alison Bartlett

ISBN 0 237 52772 3

Pig in Love
by Vivian French and Tim Archbold

ISBN 0 237 52950 5

The Donkey That Was Too Fast
by David Orme and Ruth Rivers

ISBN 0 237 52949 1

The Yellow Balloon
by Helen Bird and Simona Dimitri

ISBN 0 237 52948 3

Hamish Finds Himself
by Jillian Powell and Belinda Worsley

ISBN 0 237 52947 5

Flying South
by Alan Durant and Kath Lucas

ISBN 0 237 52946 7

Croc by the Rock
by Hilary Robinson and Mike Gordon

ISBN 0 237 52945 9

Turn off the Telly!
by Charlie Gardner and Barbara Nascimbeni

ISBN 0 237 53168 2

Fred and Finn
by Madeline Goodey and Mike Gordon

ISBN 0 237 53169 0

A Mouse in the House
by Vivian French and Tim Archbold

ISBN 0 237 53167 4

Lovely, Lovely Pirate Gold
by Scoular Anderson

ISBN 0 237 53170 4